Index

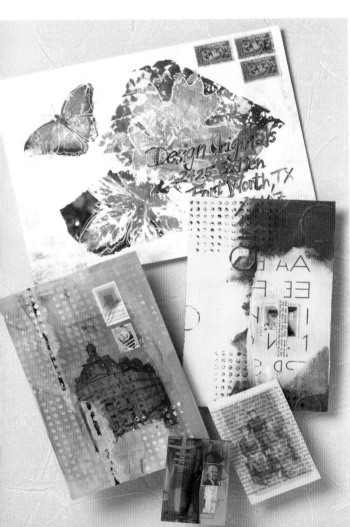

Surfaces You Can Transfer Onto

You can transfer images to basically any surface that has been primed and gessoed. It is fun and easy to transfer onto surfaces that acrylic will stick to, and that is ultimately scrubbable.

Try all of these and then try some of your own ideas!

Tyvek® Envelope

Stretched Canvas

Canvas Board

Clayboard or Cradleboard (by Ampersand)

Textured Vinyl Cover Stock

Clear Acrylic Sheet or Stamp Block

Cigar Box

Old Book Cover

'Yupo', a thin plastic similar to paper

Various Papers:

Watercolor, Acrylic, Bristol, Canvas, etc.

A note about Watercolor paper: Since Watercolor paper is made with many absorbent layers, it must be treated gently when used in the transfer process. When wet, the surface tends to get scruffy and has the potential to peel away. BE GENTLE!

A note about Acrylic paper: Acrylic paper is sized to decrease absorption, and is a good choice for beginners.

When it gets right down to it, an acrylic transfer is an interesting process in which the ink or toner on a printed paper is captured in the emulsion of a wet acrylic product and becomes bonded to the polymers when the product dries. If there was only one product to use and one kind of printed paper to use, then the process would be boring.

Excitement comes in the variations that are possible when transferring into various products or utilizing different kinds of printed materials. The outcomes are amazing along with the possibilities for embellishing transfers as part of a larger project.

Helpful Tools

Wide-blade plastic palette knives are useful for so many things. They are inexpensive and highly practical. They can be cleaned easily and don't rust. You can use this tool to spread product onto your surfaces, to spread product over printed images, to burnish the paper into the product to insure that the surface is in full contact with the wet acrylic, to scrape the paper off the back of your dried transfer, or to just paint with!

Paint scrapers, old credit or identification cards are also useful for many of the same tasks noted above, so don't fret if you can't find a palette knife!

Toothpicks are used to lift corners to start your paper peels when you begin to remove the backing.

A fine mist water spritzer is good for spraying the paper on the back of the dried transfer.

Magic Eraser Brand Sponges are absolutely fabulous for removing the last remnants of paper pulp off the back of the transfer without scratching the ink away. These are easily found in your local supermarket or superstore.

Terry Cloth Towel rubs away the little piles of pulp that build up and provides friction to remove the last fine layer that clings to the Acrylic surface.

Image of letters 'flipped' before it was transferred.

Transfer image 'flipped' after it was transferred

'Flipping' Words & Number Images

Think about images with words, text, alphabet letters and photos BEFORE you transfer them. Most computers and printers have a setting for reversing or 'flipping' an image. Remember to use this feature when appropriate... especially with numbers, words and alphabet letters.

A Few Words About Copyright Issues

So many images that attract us come from sources like magazines, books, and other printed materials. I urge you to be aware that we must respect the original writer, photographer, painter, or other artist who created the original work for us to enjoy. There are numerous places to look for images that cannot be claimed by someone else. I encourage you to take your own photos, new or vintage, and copy them for your art.

Flea markets, thrift stores, and yard sales are often good places to find old photographs that are useful for transfers. Find copyright free materials and images to use. Publications (www.doverpublications.com and www.d-originals.com) are wonderful resources for images and have many of them on CD's. Copyrights do expire but only many years after the original date of publication. As of this printing you are safe if you use books published before 1929. Once a copyright expires (and it is not renewed) the work becomes part of the "public domain" making it available for transfers. This explains why so many personal or vintage images have been utilized in this book.

If you do want to use an image you find, then I caution you to make very sure that it is not going to look like the original when you are done. You could draw a copy of part it, or trace part of it and paint it differently, then make your own color copies. When I want to use a portion of an image from a magazine, I will use only parts or pieces of the image, or transfer part of the color of an image.

I do feel comfortable using a transferred image foundation for a painting which I make over it as this allows me to change the work to a point that there is not a conflict. All art in some way is an imitation of something we see. We just need to be respectful.

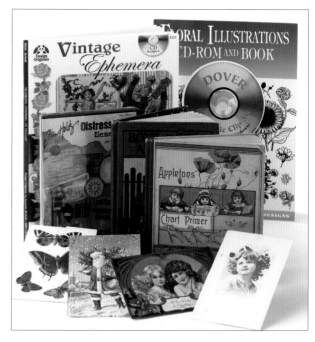

Tips Before Getting Started
About Paper Choices for Images

• **Toner or Laser prints** will make clear crisp transfers. When you are making copies at the copy shop or using your own laser printer select a mid-weight paper. The light-weight copy papers sometimes fall apart when they come in contact with the wet Acrylic products used to transfer. Note: Transfers made from inkjet prints, unless using the Digital Grounds, will be softer and a bit fuzzy.

• **Magazine images** on shiny paper will not transfer as consistently as copied images. Sometimes the inks work, sometimes they don't. Remember to read up on copyright issues when using images from magazines or books.

• **Old books**, past their copyright expiration date, usually make good transfers as do letters and ledger sheets written in real ink (not ballpoint or felt tip).

• **Exercise patience**... things take time to dry.

• **Less is more** when it comes to transfers. You don't need to glob on the products to get a good transfer.

• **Practice, practice, practice**. Learn to embrace your mistakes like I do. You will have many opportunities for using transfers that are incomplete or faulty as you practice your techniques.

Make lots of transfers, make lots of mistakes. They lead to innovations. Have lots of fun!

Setting up Your Workspace

Prepare a level working surface using a countertop or table. Cover the working surface or a large piece of cardboard with a material to which Acrylic products will not permanently adhere:

Freezer paper (be sure to use the shiny side).

Teflon craft sheets or baking sheets (be sure they are smooth, not textured).

HDPE plastic (hi-density polyethylene - plastic painter's tarps or heavy duty trash bags in at least 4 mil. thickness).

Note: It is important to have a LEVEL working surface as some of the best transfers are made with products that level themselves! So if you have a slight angle to your surface, so will your transfers!

Think Ahead...
Approach Your
Composition
Before You Begin

Any image you wish to transfer can play the central role or a supporting role in your composition. If you are creating a piece upon which the image will play the central role, then your canvas needs to be prepared up to that point.

This means that you need a Plan!

Yes, sometimes you need a plan in art. It is not always spontaneous. But don't make this more difficult than it really is. Prepare your board, paper, or canvas as you would for any other composition you are creating.

If you wish to have your image on a painted background, then do all the painting well ahead of the transfer so that the surface is dry and ready to receive the transfer.

You must then DECIDE where the transfer or multiple transfers will be placed! That's where the plan comes in. Do you want the image or images centered, off to one side, up towards the top, overlapping, vertical, or horizontal?

So many decisions must be made!

So now that you have decided where you want your image, you are ready to apply the product so that you can make your transfer!

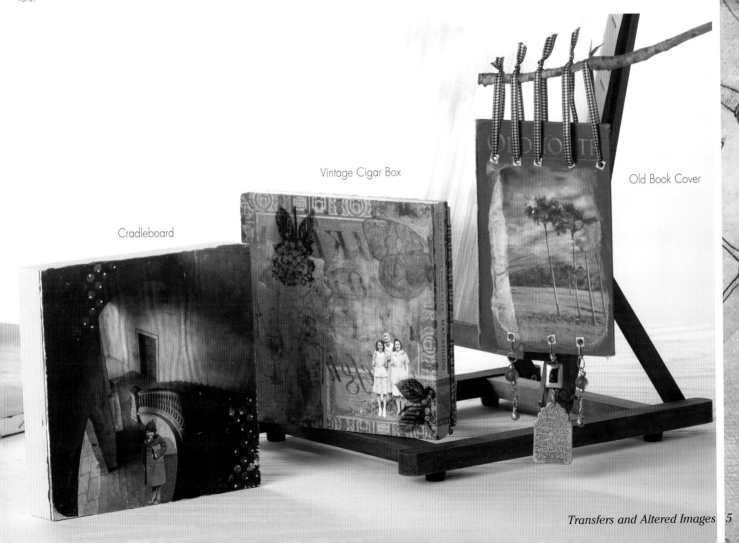

Cradleboard

Vintage Cigar Box

Old Book Cover

Acrylic Products to Make Transfers

Grandparents - Color copy (black & white setting) of vintage photo on Soft Gel (Gloss)

Utensils - Color copy on Light Molding Paste

Dad's Family - Color copy of a vintage photo on Molding Paste

Fancy Chair - Transfer on Fiber Paste

Palm Trees - Transfer on Glass Bead Gel

Suggested Products for Face to Face Transfers:

Acrylic paints and products are designed to work as a system, so combining various products on one piece of art is never a problem, nor is layering to create complex surfaces.

As a member of the Golden Artist Colors, Inc. "Working Artist" team, I am always exploring the capabilities of the various products the company manufactures. All of Golden's acrylic products are artist grade and are archival as well.

Be experimental with these products and processes.

Soft Gel, Regular Gel, Heavy Gel

Molding Paste, Light Molding Paste, Fiber Paste, Coarse Molding Paste

Glass Bead Gel, Fine Pumice Gel, Acrylic Ground for Pastels

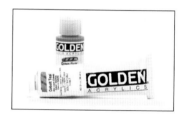

Heavy Body Paint (in tube), Fluid Acrylic Paint (in bottle)

Crackle Paste

Face - Original Image of Face from Vintage Book on Fine Pumice Gel

Pot on Table - Transfer with Tree on Acrylic Ground for Pastels

Crackle Paste

Get the best effect of a transfer on a crackled surface by applying a coat of crackle paste to a rigid surface first. Allow it to dry and crack in its own time. Paint as desired. Seal the crackled surface with a coat of Soft Gel, then do a Soft Gel (Matte or Gloss) transfer on top.

You'll get the best cracks this way. Note: A Face to Face transfer works on Crackle paste, but it won't always give you the cracks it is known for.

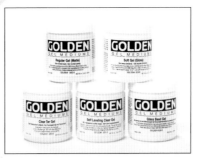

Two Faces - Tinted and Sealed on Crackle Paste

Vintage Image - Original vintage image from an old book on Pink Heavy Body Paint

Vintage Couple - on Heavy Gel (Matte) that is tinted with Fluid Acrylic color

Architecture - Image on Coarse Molding Paste

Leaves - Transfer on Transparent Pyrrole Orange Fluid Acrylic Paint

Clear Tar Gel 'skin'

Heavy Gel 'skin'

Self-Leveling Clear Gel 'skin'

Glass Bead Gel 'skin'

This involves placing the printed material to be transferred face-down into a bed of wet Acrylic product. Paper is removed from the back of the image with water after the product is dry or partially dry.

You can use designs from Toner or Laser printouts, most shiny magazine pages, scrapbook paper, and Inkjet printouts (they will be a bit fuzzy).

Using this technique allows you to utilize the broadest range of products from which to explore the transfer process, including those that do not dry clear.

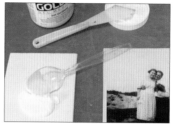

The Process ...
Making a Face-to-Face Transfer

1. Scoop out a rounded spoonful of product and plop it down in the middle part of the surface where you want to place the transfer. Here you will apply the "less is more" concept. You do not need to overload the surface with product. Judge the amount of product you need to use based on the size of the image being transferred. A teaspoon of product is good for a medium size transfer.

2. Use your palette knife or credit card to spread out the product to just beyond the area that your image will use.

It should be a smooth layer that is not thick, less than $1/16"$ is a good goal. You will find that some gels or pastes will give you a good transfer with a minimum of product and some will take more. Remove any excess product from your surface at this point. When you work with clean tools and surfaces you can just return it to its container.

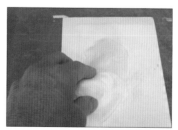

3. Place your copy of the image FACE DOWN into the product.

4. Use the edge of a clean palette knife or credit card or even the back of a plastic spoon to lightly burnish or polish the paper all over to insure that the entire area is in contact with the product. When this step is done carefully, a good quality to the transfer is insured. If you leave areas of non-contact, the transfer will be flawed, showing blank areas that have not captured the ink or toner!

5. Be careful not to get excess product on the edges or back of the paper as it will make the paper difficult to remove later. My trick for keeping things clean is to take a baby wipe and lightly wipe the back of the transfer after I have burnished it down. This will take off any excess product and provides one last rub to guarantee contact between the image and the product. This also softens the outermost layer of paper; you can almost see the image at this point.

6. Waiting: Now is the time for patience! So think about what you want to do next.

Frequently Asked Questions

How much is enough time? Waiting for paint to dry? Waiting for product to dry? Knowing just when to lift the paper off the product is the tricky part. The drying time fluctuates according to the temperature in the room, the humidity in the air, and just how thickly you applied your product. You can always lift a corner to check, but if the paper lifts too easily or is still damp, good chance it is not ready.

If, when you lift the corner, you see that your transfer has left its image on the receiving surface, then you might want to proceed by carefully lifting off the outermost layer of paper. Be careful, this is where a lot of failures can occur. Let me also say that this is where some of the best opportunities for creative discovery occur!

If you are unsure about whether enough time has passed, it's best to wait some more. Leave your transfers overnight to be safe. You'll get more "perfect" transfers and a few less "opportunities" when you wait. You can find other things to do.

When the paper is pulled away after the transfer, it leaves some residue which needs to be removed.

Gently rub the residue with your finger. It will roll off quite easily.

Soft Gel (Matte)

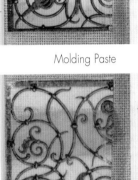

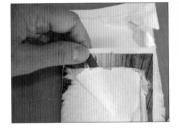

Molding Paste

Removing the Backing Paper

1. Excess paper that is not adhered to the surface will help with removal by providing you a place to grab and pull. Start by grabbing one edge of that paper and lifting off whatever will come away. If you are exceedingly lucky or have chosen a couple of products that are clearly ideal for transfers, such as Fiber Paste and Coarse Molding Paste, then much, if not all, of the paper will peel away leaving you with a fabulous transfer that is perfect or near perfect. How lucky are you?

This might not be your experience, but don't worry, you are almost there.

2. Sand the back of the paper with fine grit sandpaper to allow the water to soak in faster (optional). Use a fine mist sprayer to spray the back of the paper with water until it changes in color from white to gray signaling that the water has penetrated the paper backing.

Coarse Molding Paste

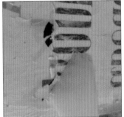

Fiber Paste

3. Wait 2-3 minutes for the water to soak through the layers of paper and then rough up the surface of the paper with your fingertip. It should begin rolling up revealing a cloudy image below. What you are doing is removing the backing of the image.

You still have a bit more work to do. Roll off all the backing and take a dry terry cloth towel and rub off the bits and pieces of paper that remain. This will allow you to see what is left to do. You should see your image captured in the surface, but it will still appear fuzzy. You will need to spritz again, give it a really good rub with the terry cloth towel to remove another layer, then dry it off and repeat until you have an almost clear image.

Let it dry for a while, then take the Magic Eraser sponge, dampened, and rub off the remaining paper residue until you have a clear image! Congratulations you have successfully transferred.

TIP: My fingers have been saved by using the towel and sponge technique.

For really tough areas you can use the flat palette knife to "shave" the excess paper off the surface. Just be sure that the surface is really wet and that you are not digging into the image with the blade.

Glass Bead Gel

Gel 'Skin' Transfers

Gel 'Skin' Transfers

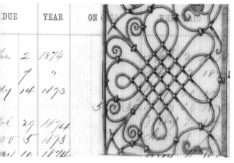

Soft Gel (Matte)

Glass Bead Gel

Regular Gel (Gloss)

Self-Leveling Clear Gel

Clear Tar Gel (tinted)

With 'skins' you will coat over the face (right side) of the printed image you wish to transfer. Use any Acrylic product that is clear or translucent when dry.

Use the product of your choice, and feel free to add a tint of Acrylic color when desired. Once the product is dry you can remove the paper off the back by wetting or soaking the 'skin' that is formed over the printed image.

Once the paper is removed you have a transparent image on the 'skin' which you can adhere or layer to another surface with a little Soft Gel (Gloss).

The Process ... Creating Gel 'Skin' Transfers

• Create Gel 'Skin' Transfers by COATING an image you wish to transfer with an acrylic product that dries either clear (transparent) or cloudy (translucent).

• Since the transparent gels and mediums that are recommended for this technique start out in a "white" state when wet, they provide a built in signal to you when the transfers are ready. The "white" disappears and you can see the images through the clear or translucent 'skin' that has formed over your image or words.

A lot of what has already been discussed applies to the Gel 'Skin' Transfer process. In this section, I will go over the areas that are different. Gel transfers are so much easier to understand because you can think of them as you would any other collage element. They are something you can add to a work in progress when you are ready. It is easy to make them in multiples and have them stored and ready for use in the future.

You will need your prepped and level work surface for the gel 'skins'.

I highly recommend using Acrylic products such as Soft Gels, Clear Tar Gel, Self-Leveling Clear Gel, or Glass Bead Gel for this process. They are all very effective, dry between transparent to translucent, and are easy to work with.

For 'skins' with the smoothest surface, use Clear Tar Gel or Self-Leveling Clear Gel.

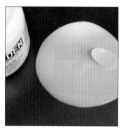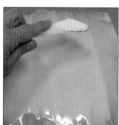

1. Lay an image out on a level working surface. I like to use cardboard covered with non-stick material so I can move it to dry.

Spread out a liberal amount of Acrylic product on top of the image.

Tip: You can do several small images, or one large image. If doing multiple images, leave enough room in between to allow for cutting them apart later.

2. Use your palette knife or a credit card to spread the Acrylic product out to a depth of $^1/16$".

3. Be sure to cover the entire image with a smooth layer.

4. Cover the entire surface of the image and go beyond the edges of the paper.

5. Allow the 'skin' to dry until it is firm to the touch and clear. Even better, allow it to dry overnight.

6. If your image is still cloudy or milky looking, this is an indication that it is not quite dry. Wait until it is completely clear. When the 'skins' are completely dry, they will peel up from the prepped work surface without any resistance. At this stage they are ready to have the paper backing removed.

7. For smaller 'skins' it is easier to drop them into a bowl of warm water and let the paper soften for 2-3 minutes, no more. The clear 'skins' may get cloudy with exposure to water, but don't worry, they will clear up again when dry.

8. When dry, these Gel 'Skin' Transfers are amazingly flexible and sturdy.

Removing the Paper from 'Skins'

On large 'skins' use the spray bottle to spritz water on the paper side and wait for it to soften. Remove as you did for the Face-to-Face transfers.

Proceed to remove the pulp as you did with the Face–to-Face transfers by rubbing, rolling off, and lightly scraping the pulp from the surface.

Applying Gel 'Skin' Transfers to Work in Progress

My approach to placement of Gel 'Skin' Transfers is just as with any other collage element. Since they are elements that can be moved around, do just that.

Decide if you want to layer the 'skin' over another visual element, or whether you want to paint it from behind or on the surface. Once you have decided what you want to do with the transfer, then all you really need is Soft Gel (Gloss) to use as the glue.

I prefer to apply a thin coat to the back of the 'skin' as well as to the surface that will receive the 'skin'. This way I am sure to have enough gel to secure the 'skin' in place. Once again, now is the time when you must be patient. Wait for the gel to turn clear before moving on to the next step.

Storing Gel 'Skins' and Transfers

Once you have cleaned and dried all of your Gel 'Skin' Transfers you can store them easily for future use. I use either clear vinyl sheet protectors or freezer wrap paper to store them on. Between each sheet I will add another sheet so that both top and bottom of the transfers are protected. Then you are able to stack and store them in a sturdy box without worry.

By making a number of transfers at a time you won't have to go through the "drying and waiting" period when you are ready to create.

This vintage words image is nearly ready. There is just a bit more paper pulp to remove from the back of the clear 'skin'.

Transparent Gel 'skins' are great for layering. There are three 'skins' in this photo: the words, the face, and the color.

Gel 'Skin' Transfers can be easily cut and trimmed with scissors to fit into your composition.

Fun Applications

The large image of the bridge and the vintage image of the little boy were transferred with the "quick" method on a painted canvas board.

Quick-Drying Soft Gel Transfers

So you want to transfer but you don't have all day or all night. Well there is one product that will give you almost immediate good quality results and that is Soft Gel (Gloss). You can use Matte or Semi-gloss, but the quickest is the Gloss.

Follow the directions for any Face-to-Face Transfer, but when it comes to the "waiting for things to dry" part, start checking after only 5 or so minutes, especially if the weather in your room or studio is warm and dry.

Remember that drying time of Acrylic products is affected by the weather. You will know if your transfer has occurred when the face of the paper remains adhered to the surface and the only the backing paper comes up.

If when you check your transfer, the image is still clearly visible on the paper, then put it down and burnish once again, waiting a couple of minutes more. The trick is to be sure you have burnished down the image you wish to transfer into an evenly distributed coat of the Soft Gel.

Quickly you will have a very good transfer on many kinds of surfaces. I recommend that you practice a few times to get your timing down.

Small Clear Stamp Blocks

Most rubber stamp stores have Acrylic Stamp Mounts available for sale. They are thick blocks of Acrylic that have either a beveled edge on one side or plain edges all around. I especially like the beveled edge mounts for this project.

These make wonderful paperweights, appreciated gifts, and memorable displays for your favorite photos.

Materials: Soft Gel (Gloss), Fluid Acrylic Paint (in bottles), and Heavy Body Paint (in tubes).

Stamp, Collage or Transfer - 1. Acrylic Stamp Mounts are wonderful for their intended purpose, but I recognized their potential for miniature paper-weights and collages the moment I laid my eyes upon them in my favorite Rubber Stamp Store. They come in numerous sizes and are delightful as gifts. • 2. Start by selecting an image (Use StazOn ink to stamp an image) or in this case I used a photo image that is a good size for the mount. Hold it up to check how it looks. • 3. For either a Collage or a Transfer version, you begin by applying Soft Gel (Gloss) to the picture side of the paper. This is important. You are making a reverse composition, so the first thing you will see when you look at the final piece is the main image. • 4. Wipe off all excess gel from the surface of the paper and the mount. An alcohol wipe or a baby wipe is great for removing excess paint on Plexiglas surfaces. Let the image dry.

Adding Color - 5. If you wish to make the image a transparent transfer, remove the paper backing by wetting it with water and rubbing. If you don't want it transparent, then leave the paper backing on the image. • 6. Start applying color using your palette knife or brush to color various areas of the stamp mount on the same side as the image. Apply a couple of coats of Fluid Acrylic colors or one coat of Heavy Body Paint colors. • 7. To create lines and patterns, draw through the wet paint with a color shaper tool or with the end of your paintbrush. Just wipe off the extra periodically or you may just be putting it back where you started! • 8. Check once in a while to see how it looks. You might find you need a pop of strong color somewhere for that last touch.

By now you have noticed that I like transparent things... Fluid Acrylic Paints in transparent colors, transparent gels, transparencies, in fact this whole book is really about seeing through layers.

Painting on Plexiglas is enjoyable because the clear surface really reveals the transparent qualities of the colors. I love the look of see-through layers hanging in a window.

Clear Plexiglas Sheets

Larger Plexiglas compositions can be really interesting. The colors and layers are amazing. I was pleased with the transfers and I hope you will try your own hand at these surfaces as well.

Note: Leave the protective sheet on the front of the Plexiglas until completely finished. This prevents excess paint or product from getting on the front.

Tip: If you find that you have a bit of paint where you don't want it, take a little alcohol on a paper towel and rub away the excess paint to clean up the surface.

2 Fish - (Blue, green, and red), painted with Fluid Acrylics
Evelyn - (3 faces) with yarn tassels transfers then painted with Fluid Acrylics and Heavy Body Acrylics.

My Mom & Friends - To create the hanging Plexiglas constructions on this page, I used a Crop-O-Dile tool to punch perfect holes in the sheets of Plexi. The various pieces are joined together with wire, beads and ribbons for embellishments.

Working on Plexiglas Sheets - 1. Remember to remove the protective sheet from the side you will be transferring on. Don't laugh, it happens!
2. For Collage and Transfer images, apply Soft Gel (Gloss) to the front of the image, then place them onto the Plexiglas surface, following the directions for a face-to-face transfer (pages 8 - 9). I used a small vintage photo and some lace elements for the blue area.
3. Allow to dry. Clean the pulp off the transfers to reveal the images (or Use StazOn ink to stamp an image).
4. Apply areas of Fluid Acrylic Paint colors and Heavy Body Acrylic Paint colors to the same side as the transfers. This allows me to work all the processes on one side only and keep the "front" side clean and pristine. I removed some of the paint with the end of a paintbrush to create the lines. (There will be more on this process later in the book!)
5. Here is the front of the Plexiglas after it has been painted, and before being combined with the other pieces to make the hanging.

Stacked Transfers and Layering

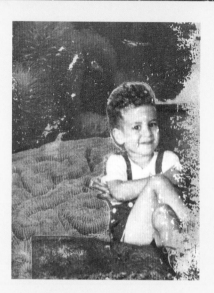

I wanted to give a vintage photo of my husband as a little boy a "surreal" background and do it all as a transfer.

Approach this technique from an inside-out point of view. Working backwards, figure out which image should be placed first.

Cut out the foreground image and place it face down in the Acrylic product, lining it up on one corner for a Face-to-Face transfer. Apply the background image to the entire open area, overlapping the foreground image where needed.

Burnish down both images at the same time, being sure to remove any air bubbles, and wait for things to dry. After a little touch up with Fluid Acrylic Colors, the final outcome was cute and playful!

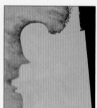

1. Here is the background piece I chose for my whimsical composition. After a little touch up with Fluid Acrylic colors, the final outcome was cute and playful, and just what I wanted.
2. I covered the entire board with the background image including the image of my husband. I rubbed the entire surface evenly with my palette knife to be sure that all air bubbles were gone and it was smooth.
3. Start embellishing by applying acrylic product to the entire board. In a stacked transfer it will be necessary to closely trim the image that will be in the foreground when the piece is complete. The subsequent images can be placed on top of the first image.

REMEMBER to avoid getting wet product on the back of the first image. Remove each layer separately.

Face to Face

I playfully named this piece to reflect the process as well as the subject matter. This familiar classic image was cut in half and transferred onto the surface of the inside of an Ampersand Clayboard or Cradleboard Shadow Box using Soft Gel (Gloss). It gave the illusion that each figure was trying to see the other.

I proceeded to pull out various other images and pieces of text to build up a transferred background for the empty spaces between the two faces. With the exception of color added with Fluid Acrylics, there are no elements on this piece except transfers! Of which there are many!

Climbing Up

This small Ampersand Clayboard or Cradleboard was just right for an image of a spiral staircase. Numerous overlapping images create the background of the final piece and incorporate the three women.

The one at the rear is a transfer, the middle one is a reverse painted 'faux' transfer using a transparency, and the third one is collaged in place.

Overlapping Transfers

For the Overlapping Transfers technique, start with a "naked" surface (primed or gessoed white) and transfer a large area of printed words or loose line drawings Face-to-Face into one kind of Acrylic product.

Use something absorbent for this first coat so that it can be flooded with wet Fluid Acrylic paints for color later on. Allow the transfer to dry and remove and clean the transfer of all traces of paper backing.

Now select another image (or several) that fit with the first. Choose an additional product, things that are translucent would be good choices.

Decide upon placement, apply the product and make your transfers. Be sure that you overlap your images so that you can see the first one.

Once dry and cleaned, you can paint the surface with watered down Fluid Acrylic paint using transparent pigments. Overlap your colors, mop and rub the surface to get the effect you want. You can lay in some areas of color full strength as well. Stop when you are pleased with the surface.

Allow it to dry thoroughly. The last set of transfers will be done on Soft Gel (Gloss). Choose your last images and decide on placement. Be sure that you have the underlying elements just as you want them because once the Soft Gel is on any of the surface area, it will lock in the color underneath. Apply the Soft Gel, create the transfer, and clean the surface. Add any additional elements to complete your composition and you are done.

Tip: You may continue to add additional transfers on top of your painted areas as well.

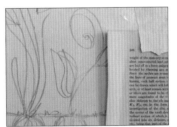
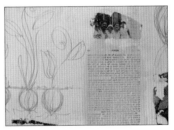

Materials: Use something absorbent… Light Molding Paste or Fiber Paste for the first coat. Choose something translucent for additional coats… Soft Gel (translucent and glossy), Heavy Gel (translucent and matte) or Coarse Molding Paste (translucent and a bit gritty) would be good choices.
1. Place your first graphite pencil drawing into the Fiber Paste on the stretched canvas.
2. Clean up the graphite transfers and place several vintage book pages into Coarse Molding Paste.
3. Remove the pulp from all the transfers and assess what to do next.

4. COLOR! Start by laying in some areas of Titan Buff Fluid Acrylic to bring the color of the vintage book pages in line with the empty areas of the canvas. You will notice that the color of the old pages actually transfers as well as the text. Then on to washes into the Coarse Molding Paste with Fluid Manganese Blue Hue, some Sap Green and Pyrrole Red as well, along with a bit of this and that.
5. At this point my Botanical artist friend, Sally Markell, came for a visit and I asked her to create a pencil drawing of a radish that we could transfer into Soft Gel (Matte). Here is the outcome of the transferred drawing.
6. Paint in the details of the drawing, using watercolor techniques with Fluid Acrylics
7. Here is the final radish: Remember it is a hand-painting of a transferred line drawing over a Coarse Molding Paste transfer of a vintage book page.

Painted Gel 'Skin' Transfers

I love change and look for opportunities to make something look different whenever I can. By painting the back side of a gel 'skin' transfer, you can remake the image over and over again.

This process works best with black and white or sepia toned images.

Colors of Fluid Acrylic paints and Clear Tar Gel

Girl in a Blue Dress

The central images (the postcard and the girl in a blue dress) for this mixed media piece are painted gel 'skins'.

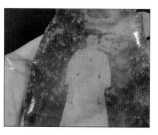 

Tinted Photos

1. Here is a Gel 'Skin' Transfer made from a vintage image. It is ok, but I wanted the figure to command more interest.
2. Add a bit of color to the back side of the image. Use Titan Buff Fluid Acrylic to tint the face and body parts of the image. Then add some color to the dress. Look closely for any details like a rose bush, then tint the roses too.

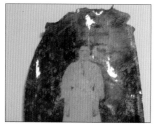 

3. The close up view show the colors on the rough 'skin'.
4. A close up after it has been added as a collage element.

Note: Embellish the front surface of any 'skin' transfers as well! If you want to bring out details in an image, try highlighting details with Fluid Acrylic colors using a small brush. It's fun and makes a lot of difference in the outcome.

Limon on Canvas

Since the Gel 'Skin' Transfers are made with Acrylic products, a transfer of a simple drawing can be embellished with Fluid Acrylic colors. The Transparent colors I used were Hansa Yellow Medium and Sap Green Hue.

These colors really enhanced the image, making it stand out against the other collage elements on the board without sacrificing any of the transparent qualities that transfer 'skins' offer.

You'll need a 12" x 12" canvas board, collage materials, Clear Tar Gel and Soft Gel (Gloss) for Acrylic transfer 'skins', a drawing and a paintbrush.

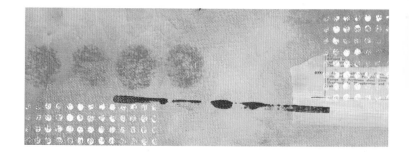

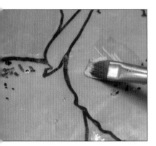

on - 1. Here is a large Clear
Gel "skin" transfer made from a
he drawing on heavy tracing
per.

Add Fluid Acrylic Hansa Yellow
dium paint to the lemons. Use a
of Sap Green and Green Gold
he leaves.

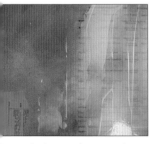

Here is the painted Skin Transfer.

To apply the transfer to a col-
ed and painted canvas, spread
in layer of Soft Gel (Gloss) to the
ace using a palette knife.

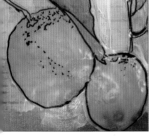

Place the transfer and burnish the
es down with a palette knife.
r add the words and remainder
details.

Mixed-Up Media:

When I teach classes in transfer techniques, I usually encourage students to put several different products on one board and transfer some "related" images into the various products. By related, I mean something that together in a completed piece will "hang together" visually or tell a story.

All the painting and embellishing is done after the images have been transferred. This is a good way to dis-cover the nature of the various products and how they behave.

The trick to the process is making an "artful" choice of images and understanding where to place them. By paint-ing and embellishing at the end you can see how to trans-form your transfers with the addition of transparent color, additional collage elements, and some well-placed camou-flage. At the end, a unifying coat of transparent or translu-cent medium will even out any surface discrepancies.

Family

Several pieces of colored images were randomly transferred into Light Molding Paste to create a background. A vintage photo was collaged and painted details were added.

Eye & Two Hands

The 'skin' transfer pieces are on Fine Pumice Gel, enhanced with color washes using Fluid Acrylic colors after drying.

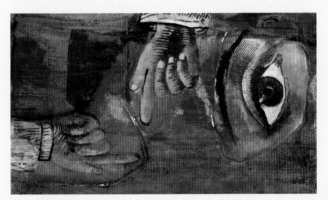

Bird Nest

An image of lace and sky was created by photo-copying an actual piece of old lace with an image of a blue sky placed over it. This image was transferred into Light Molding Paste along with snippets of old text.

The collage was done with an actual piece of a vintage foreign letter onto the surface.

To add color, I painted and embellished the surface with Fluid Acrylic Manganese Blue washes.

When all of that was thoroughly dry, a bird's nest image was transferred onto the painted surface into Coarse Molding Paste and embellished with Fluid Acrylic colors to create a hand-paint-ed look.

Layered Gel 'Skin' Transfers

One of the most fun things to do is to create layered images with your gel 'skin' transfers. Take a 'skin', find another image or some great words, overlap them and you have a unique image you could not have found ready made.

Bunch of Kids - I made a 'skin' transfer of this great photo of a bunch of kids from times past.

I love how it looks like someone gathered the children all in the back yard and snapped the photo.

A Happy Home - I happened upon the best page in an old book: A Happy Home! With the "bunch of kids" image layered over the words, it started to tell me a story of happy days and times.

It is wonderful when serendipity plays a role in our art!

A Happy Home

Tint the Photo - As an option, tint the photo 'skin' with Fluid Acrylic colors to use on another composition.

When you have a number of prepared Gel 'Skin' Transfers on hand, it is easy for you to put together a composition along with other elements you have in your supplies. I like using Canvas Boards to create these colorful "stories". Their small size makes them ideal to prop up on an easel for inspiration or to enjoy in a frame.

You can take it one step further by making a number of colorful backgrounds on one day and gel skins on another day. When you are ready, you can devote one day to assembling as many as you wish! What fun is that!

Considering all the materials you already have in your art stash, you can really take your ideas to the next level by incorporating transfers of all kinds into your work. Sometimes I can spend half a day trying out different elements before I finally glue it down, but on other days a composition will come together in a flash! A background, a gel transfer layered over words, some Soft Gel ...

Since the Gel 'Skin' Transfers are transparent, you can layer them over other words or images to get a more complex image. Just remember, treat your Gel 'Skin' Transfers as transparent collage elements and try them out on various backgrounds to see where they can best be used. Sometimes combinations of vintage with contemporary are very exciting and surprising.

Working with Words, Text & Numbers

Apply the same rules for the kinds of images that will transfer as you would for Face-to-Face transfers. The need to "reverse" the image is not as critical, because you can always apply the product to the correct side of the image and get exactly what you see, no reversals, since you are working with "see-through" products.

It is easy to work with words, text, alphabet letters, numbers or schematics when doing the Gel Transfer process.

HINT: Don't trim your image too closely. Leave a little area around the image that will remain after you have burnished. This will assist in lifting the paper off after the image has transferred.

Here is the Caution: Since gel 'skins' are not attached to a rigid receiving surface, they can distort or stretch during the stage in which the paper is removed. Take care to work gently when removing the paper backing. You can use the towel and sponge method as long as you are gentle. You will be rewarded with crystal clear (or frosted if you used Matte gels) transfers ready for your next piece of art.

Layered Transfers

Create layered images with your stash of transfers. Here is a pretty stretched canvas with layers of images and textures.

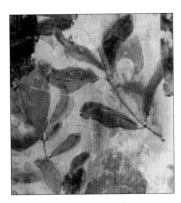

Close ups showing the various layers of blossoms. Some are Face-to-Face transfers while others are Gel 'Skin' Transfers.

Blue Jay

This 12" x 16" board has seven different kinds of transfers incorporated onto one surface! Some are 'skins', some are face-to-face, and some are 'faux'. There is a snippet of transparency film as well. The challenge is to make it all work together.

Pomegranate Nights

I am a great believer in reusing things that have been used before and using everything you have. This piece started as another painting. I kept some of the colors that were on it and painted over what I didn't like. I added some Crackle Paste as well, staining and sealing it with a coat of Soft Gel before I added any transfers.

The first layer of transfers was old images from my friend, Sally. I made Face-to-Face transfers into Soft Gel (Gloss) over the Crackle Paste using copies of pomegranate blossoms.

On the side I was making a set of Acrylic 'Skin' Transfers using the same images. I added some small transfer images of blue lanterns and when they were all cleaned up I placed my cleaned and ready pomegranate 'skin' transfers on the surface, gluing them down with Soft Gel (Gloss).

I poured a coat of Clear Tar Gel over the entire surface when everything was dry. While the Clear Tar Gel was still wet I stamped areas of dots with Matte Fluid Green Gold and larger circles with Quinacridone Red.

The contrast of shiny Clear Tar Gel Surface and the Matte paint is great.

Childhood Memories

The background was collaged and painted with Titan Buff to provide texture and interest. A copy of a painting done by Sally Markell was cut out and transferred onto the background using Soft Gel (Gloss). Once clean and dry, the surface was treated with a wash of Quinacridone Magenta Fluid Acrylics mixed with water.

The image of the girl is a Regular Gel (Matte) 'skin' of a vintage postcard image. The final details are added using a Sharpie Poster Pen.

Handmade Book with Transparency Accents

Images and words printed on clear transparency film add a great look and shiny texture to handmade books and altered books. Add a layered image to the cover for a great look. Print a texture on a transparency sheet, then paint the back of the sheet brown for an easy bookmark. Add a pretty butterfly layer with transparent wings. And finally, collage an image of a child on an orange colored page and watch the color glow through the transparency sheet.

How fun is it that we can take any image, words or photo and make a transparency of it almost immediately! On your next trip to a local copy shop take along some of your favorite images and a few "copier" quality transparency sheets (Not Inkjet) and try them out.

When you copy color or vintage photos on a black and white copier you get high contrast images that are less detailed but very interesting. By copying vintage photos with a color copier you will keep the exact nuance of color that the photograph reveals. I think words and line drawings are best done on a black and white copier, not a color one.

Of course with transparency images, they are all "see-through" so you can take advantage of this when layering them in your work.

Images on Transparency Film
"Little Snippets of Transparency Film ... Alternative"

Little snippets of transparency film can add just the right "touch" to a collage, mixed media project or scrapbook page. Don't overlook this handy alternative.

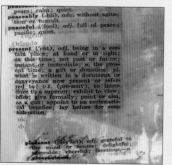

Don't forget to look on the backs of vintage postcards. There is nothing like the little stories that you can find. I frequently glean through mine and make transparencies of the stories I like best. They make great additions to collages as 'faux' transfers.

Here is that same image of children I used earlier, but this time as a transparency. I layered it three times: First over words, then over a piece of painted transparency film, then over a photo of clouds.

Here are some excerpts from a vintage dictionary photocopied onto transparency film. I love to add them to pieces I am working on.

An image of palm trees and sky is layered over words. The effect is subtle and nice.

'Faux' Transparency Sheet Transfers

In addition to the two kinds of transfers we have discussed, we will be covering 'faux' transfer processes which will use transparencies, transparent papers, Plexiglas collages, and gel 'skins' combined with your favorite rubber stamps.

Fluid Acrylic color: Titan Buff

Call to Dinner -

Stacked transfer on a 9" x 12" canvas embellished with Fluid Acrylic colors.

Written in Stone - This 12" x 12" canvas was covered entirely with Coarse Molding Paste into which several copies and pages were transferred in the Face-to-Face method (pages 8 - 9). The roughness of the paste is smoothed down by the transfer process so the texture on the canvas surface varies between smooth and rough. Fluid Acrylic colors were used to create subtle color washes over this entire surface after the transfers were completed.

A transparency film of a vintage photo and hand-drawn color-pencil images of poppy seed heads are layered over the text words and collaged onto the surface.

Paint Areas -
Isolate small areas by painting the BACK of a transparency sheet with Titan Buff, especially behind words, text and faces.

To avoid losing the details of faces and other important elements in your black and white transparencies, or of vintage photos in sepia tones, just use a little Titan Buff Fluid Acrylic on the back of the film to make faces or other details more opaque and visible.

You can also tint the Titan Buff with any color to add opaque details to other areas on your transparency.

Mixed Media Canvas -

I began this 12" x 12" canvas piece with the intention of transferring blocks of color and line rather than images. I selected pieces of color copies that had these elements and transferred them onto the surface using Soft Gel (Gloss).

It turned out that they resembled doors and windows so I incorporated that idea into the development of the piece by adding 'skins' made with Glass Bead Gel to the surface.

I also added a back-painted transparency (see instructions above) and a 'faux' transfer 'skin' to support the linear elements of window openings, along with pieces of an old letter.

I enhanced the color with additional layers of Fluid Acrylic colors.

New Ways to Create Transparent Layers in Mixed Media Art

A really wonderful 'faux' transfer effect utilizes the transparent qualities of tissue-type papers to create the look of a transparency but with hand-copied images. You will need heavy duty tissue paper (not the thin kind), Silk tissue, Glassine sheets (a heavy tracing paper that doesn't wrinkle when collaged), or unwaxed sandwich wrap paper.

The last option is really inexpensive and sturdy and I use it a lot. Look for it in your restaurant supply or bulk food supplier.

How to Use Tissue

Here is what you do. Trace or draw an image onto the paper using a permanent ink pen or India ink. Cut out the image leaving ?" to ?" of white area showing. Once you have prepared your receiving background, adhere these drawings to the surface of your work with Soft Gel (Gloss or Matte).

Once they are dry, they can be painted and glazed with transparent color, which further allows the image to blend into the surface.

Here is a simple drawing of a Blue Jay on Glassine Paper. If you are not an accomplished drawer (and I am not), then trace images you like from copyright free sources or your own photographs.

For this drawing I used tissue paper and collaged it with Soft Gel (Gloss).

Add these 'Faux' Transfers on top of your Face-to-Face transfers without a problem. Just use a lightweight gel such as Soft Gel to apply them. Be gentle during the application so as not to tear the transfer. When dry, you can paint the transfer and blend it into the background. The tissue just disappears and becomes texture.

This bird is a simple line drawing made with India ink on Glassine. I later cut it out and applied it to a canvas.

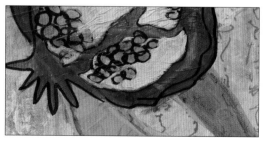

The nicest thing about the 'faux' transfer process is the ease with which you decide on placement.

You can continue to move around your images until you are satisfied with the placement.

You can work large or small as well.

The two parrots, the woman, and the leaves are all separate 'faux' transfers. Because they are lightweight, you can easily layer them without building up a lot of bulk.

A Work in Progress

Good compositions evolve over time. Often it works best to begin with simple background techniques and just let things happen. Usually the background colors and design elements will influence the images on the piece.

Follow the progress of this piece and you will see what I mean.

Birds on Blue - This small canvas began with layers of collaged vintage papers and Titan Buff Fluid Acrylic Paint (a really good match to old paper). Some bird images were drawn onto sturdy tissue paper (glassine paper and deli wrap paper works as well) and applied with Soft Gel (Gloss). When dry I washed in some Manganese Blue Hue Fluid Acrylic Paint over the background except for the birds.

I wiped away some of the paint to make the paint uneven. I then embellished the birds with applications of transparent colors of Fluid Acrylic Paint and lastly added circles of Interference Paint.

Here are the steps I take in developing a piece using 'Faux' Transfers on tissue paper:

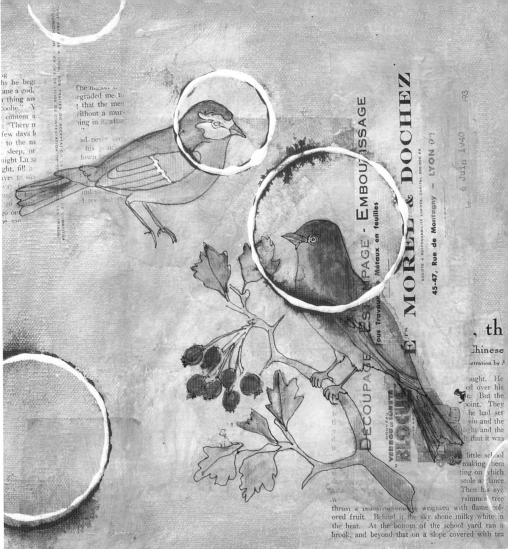

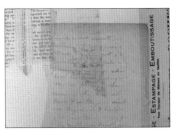 

1. Prepare a canvas by first collaging various vintage papers onto the surface with Soft Gel (Gloss).
2. Unify the various whites by adding some Fluid Acrylic Titan Buff to the canvas as it is a good mimic for old vintage pages, and then add the tissue paper drawings using Soft Gel (Gloss).

Layers of Images -

A drawing of a bird, acrylic paints, pastel chalk colors, and transferred words decorate this art done on smooth watercolor paper.

The final details you see on the painting were added after I could assess how the composition was developing.

It is good to stop and take a look ever so often. Remember sometimes less is more!

3. Wash in areas of Fluid Acrylic color. I used Manganese Blue Hue mixed with Polymer Medium to create the first layer of color. I still want the papers to show, but pushed into the background more.
4. Continue to add color with other Blues in Fluid Acrylic colors.
5. Add color to the transfers of the birds with transparent Fluid Acrylic colors. I like Indian Yellow Hue, Sap Green, Quinacridone Burnt Orange, Quinacridone/Nickel Azo Gold, and Quinacridone Red for example.

Take what you learned about making a Gel 'Skin' Transfer and leave out the paper part. Yes, leave out the paper or images. Make a clear 'skin' out of Clear Tar Gel or Self Leveling Clear Gel, or any of the transparent products and let it turn clear. Then take out your favorite rubber stamp images, use StazOn Ink and stamp a 'faux' transfer image.

Better yet, tint the product before you pour it and you'll have a colored 'skin'.

Even better, tint stamped images with transparent Fluid Acrylic Colors and see them come alive. When the paint is dry you will be able to use these stamped Gel 'skins' as collage elements.

Mushroom Altered Book Page - Print a digital image of mushrooms onto dry 'skin' that has been treated with Digital Ground Clear. While the image is still a bit tacky, transfer it into the book by coating the page with a very thin even layer of Soft Gel (Gloss).

Clear Tar Gel
Self-Leveling Clear Gel

Altered Book Pages - Embellish and alter pages with 'Faux Skins' to add color, texture and images to the overall look.

Prime a Page - Prime a page in an old book with Fluid Acrylic color. Use Titan Buff to mask some of the text.
Adding Color - A book page made a good place for 'faux skin' transfers to find a home. Continue to add color to an image, highlighting the details.
'Faux Skin' - 1. On a level covered workspace spread a thin even layer of Self-Leveling Clear Gel, allowing it to dry.

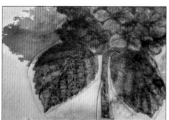

2. When the skin is dry it will be totally clear. At this point you can peel it off the HDPE without difficulty.
3. Stamp the surface of a stamp using StazOn®. Be sure to press down straight and firm. The skin is slick and the stamp can slide.
4. Paint the back of this Stamped 'Faux Skin' transfer.
5. By layering it over a background with a water media effect, you can enhance the colors of the hydrangea stamp.

Add Iridescent Color

Try embellishing a 'skin' stamped with an ornate image using Iridescent Fluid Acrylic colors. These paints really look like the metals they are named after. Here I used the Bronze.

Add Fluid Acrylic Colors

Add more Fluid Acrylic colors. The transparent look will let the stamp show through and add beautiful variations to the colors.

Beat the Clock - I created a background using various Face-to-Face transfers, areas of texture with Crackle Paste, and Fluid Acrylic Paint. 'Faux Skin' transfers that have the clock face stamp and the Admit One ticket stamp were added. A coat of Self-Leveling Clear Gel at the end unifies the surface.

Additional 'Faux Skin' Applications

Great for cards, altered books, ATCs and as collage elements, for layering!

1. If you want a colored 'skin' it is easy to do. Add 1-3 drops of transparent Fluid Acrylic Color to 2-3 teaspoons of Self-Leveling Clear Gel and mix thoroughly.
2. Once you mix the color, let the gel rest until any air bubbles have dissipated. The color will seem pastel at this stage, but remember the gel will dry clear.
3. Spread tinted gel out on your covered level workspace.

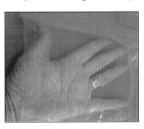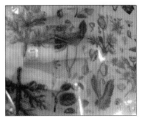

4. Here is the tinted 'skin'.
5. Here is the tinted 'skin' after being stamped with Brown StazOn Ink.
6. The tinted 'skin' can be layered over different colors to introduce more color or pattern.

Turquoise Chair - Inkjet transfer into Soft Gel (Gloss) on a transferred and painted background

Home computers and printers play an increasingly important role in our "art-making" activities. We almost all own a digital camera, frequently modify images, and use word-processing programs endlessly. Maximizing the affordable technologies we already own is important to us.

Here are some simple techniques and some new Golden products that will help to do just that. Your art-making capabilities are about to soar.

Inkjet Transfers

The clearest and sharpest transfers result when we use toner or laser copies to make them. BUT, inkjet transfers are fun and easy to make and provide a softer look overall. There are a number of ways that you can make them. I will share a few of them.

Face-To-Face Inkjet Into Soft Gel

This is quick and easy. Follow all of the directions for a Face-to-Face transfer using Soft Gel (Gloss) as your medium. Then use an image you have sized and printed on your inkjet printer and apply and burnish it as directed.

Check the speed at which your particular ink will transfer by lifting the corner of your transfer and checking the image. If it is not ready, just burnish it back down and wait a few more minutes. You can usually lift the paper off in almost one piece leaving behind a "ghost" image on the paper. The transferred image is a bit fuzzy, but totally "artistic".

The Best Part

The best part is that you can play with the color and contrast in your photo editing program and get some very interesting images. Make a series and see how many variations you can do. This is a good process for those of you who want to transfer into journals and books. Just be sure to put a piece of cardboard covered in waxed or freezer paper behind your pages so the product doesn't wet the pages below.

You must lift quickly you so won't have all that backing paper scraping to do, as your pages won't tolerate it.

Soft Gel (Gloss)

Bubble-Up -

This delightful Fish composition was made by transferring three images of fish printed on an Inkjet Printer. I used Soft Gel (Gloss) to transfer the images onto the painted surface. Inkjet transfers are not always crisp. Since I was doing an "underwater" scene, I just took advantage of the softer, fuzzier quality of this transfer process.

Painted bubble details and a little embellishment of the fish was all it needed.

Inkjet Transparency Transfers

1. This is a photograph I took in a bog in South Florida. A wild Iris is so beautiful to see in person. I use this image repeatedly when I teach because I want people to think of using their own digital images to make art.

2. The second image is the transfer I made using the process described.

3. What a horizon!

4. Here the transfer is enhanced with a bit of pastel pencil. Note the dotted quality of the transfer image, which results from the beads of ink deposited on the film during printing.

Inkjet On Transparency Film

This Transfer process requires the use of Non-Inkjet transparency film. Select your image, adjust for color and size. Nearby have a piece of smooth Bristol paper and a wide blade palette knife or credit card. Print out your image onto the surface of the transparency. You will actually see the ink sitting on the surface of the film.

Carefully flip the transparency film over onto the Bristol paper and burnish the wet ink onto the surface. Lift off and there is your image. The resulting image will have a speckled effect that is a result of all those beads of ink. These are great when you embellish them with colored pencils or pastel pencils.

Digital Mixed Media Applications

As I promised, something completely new and a real collaboration between digital media, such as your home computer and inkjet printer, and the art world: Digital Mixed Media Products from Golden Artist Colors, Inc. It takes a bit of processing to wrap your mind around the possibilities, but once you start, there is no turning back.

I want to share with you some exciting ways to use your home computer and inkjet printer to create art, including making transfers. For those of us that are "of the moment" in our working habits, running out to the copy store to get something copied isn't always convenient. Golden Artist Colors has come out with a line of Digital Grounds which are quite amazing as to what they allow inkjet printers to print upon.

In the past, the problem with inkjet printers has been that the inks, being water-based, don't print equally well on every surface that can be fed through your home printer. In some cases the inks bleed too much and seep through the paper, making blotches. In other cases the inks just bead up on the surface not soaking in at all.

Up until now, these problems have limited the ability to use our printers to make "digital" prints on anything that was not specifically formulated for use in an inkjet printer. That meant the use of transparencies, canvas, watercolor papers, art papers, or even thin sheets of metal or wood was out of the question, unless you paid extra for the ones that were "made for inkjet printers."

Using Your Home Computer with Digital Grounds

Digital Grounds
Digital Grounds -
Clear, White and Non-Porous
Gel Topcoat w/UVLS

Digital Grounds are an exciting product! They provide a way to get around surface problems. Use these products to help add exciting and unusual surfaces to your art.

Versatile digital compatible products work by providing a surface coating that creates a film on almost any item. This clear film captures inkjet inks before they actually get to the paper. This allows you to bypass the problems of ink absorption.

With a little prep work, metallic specialty papers, aluminum foil, thin metal sheets (copper for example), Mylar, Lexan, Plexiglas, acetate, plastic, Yupo, paint skins, thin wood sheets... in fact nearly any paper, foil or surface that can safely travel through a home printer can be prepared to accept transfers.

Digital Ground products provide the opportunity for you to create both 'faux' transfers and actual transfers.

Use Digital Ground Products for Printing

There are three kinds of Digital Grounds: Clear (Gloss), White (Matte), and Clear for Non-Porous Surfaces.
All are sold in liquid form and are easily applied to the surface of whatever you want to run through your inkjet printer. Determine in advance what thickness level your printer can tolerate before running anything through. This process works best with printers that have either a straight paper path (ideal), or an "L-shape" paper path, not "S" feeds.

Check out the details of the process on www.goldenpaints.com for all of the technical information you could possibly need. This site contains information on printer compatibility and techniques.

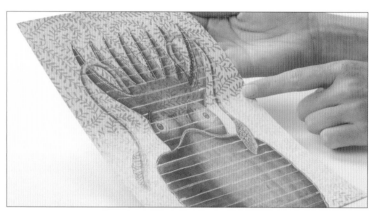

Prepare a Printable Surface

Clear and White Digital Grounds are fully compatible with a variety of papers, the only difference being that one dries clear, and one dries white and matte (but not totally opaque).

Giant Squid

This photo demonstrates the difference between the Clear and White Digital Grounds. This highly porous patterned paper was coated with Clear and with White Grounds. The image was then printed on an ink-jet printer. Note how the pattern recedes on the side where the White Ground has been applied. Additional embellishments were made to the image using archival pens and Fluid Interference Color.

Printing on Non-porous Surfaces

When printing on non-porous surfaces such as metal, plastic, Yupo, paint skins, wood sheets, etc... use Digital Ground for Non-Porous Surfaces.

Digital Mixed Media Transfer Processes

Use an Inkjet printer and home computer.

Transparency Sheet Transfers on Non-Inkjet Transparency Film

In the process on page 27, Inkjet onto Transparency Film, I commented that the resulting transfer was "dotted" due to the beads of ink on the surface of the transparency film. The application of two cross-brushed coats of the Digital Ground for Non-Porous Surfaces to the surface of the transparency film makes a HUGE difference in the clarity of the transfer. Here is the process.

• Select the digital image that you wish to transfer, adjust the contrast, then size and orient it in your photo editing program.

• Prepare a **Non-Inkjet Transparency sheet** with the Digital Ground for Non-Porous Surfaces allowing it to dry completely after each coat.

• Place the prepared transparency sheet into your inkjet printer and print on "best photo" option.

• The inks are captured in the digital ground and you have a beautiful transparency of your image.

But you aren't done yet. Now you will want to transfer that image.

Transferring a Transparency Image

Place a transparency image ink side down on dampened paper. Using your palette knife, a credit card, or other burnishing tool, firmly burnish the surface of the transparency film, transferring the image to the paper. You can feel comfortable rubbing hard for this method. Lift one corner to check the progress of the transfer. If there is still a lot of "image" left on the film, drop the film back in place and continue to burnish, until all or most of the ink has transferred to the paper.

You will need to "fix" this transferred image with Archival Varnish or Digital Media Gel Topcoat before any additional embellishments can be made. You may reuse your transparency film after washing it thoroughly with soap and water.

1. Dampen a piece of Block Printing paper (or other absorbent smooth face paper) with a bit of water and allow it to sit for a few minutes. Note: Be sure that the paper is dampened in the area you wish to transfer.
2. Place a transparency sheet on the dampened paper with the image ink side down.
3. Burnish thoroughly, and lift. The image transfers to the paper like magic.
Note: Prepare transparency sheets with Digital Ground Clear. Remember to mark the back side with a piece of tape. This will help you remember that the ink side (non-tape) goes through the printer. Allow them to dry. Print your desired images from your inkjet printer and home computer.

Some of the Surfaces that Can Be Utilized with Digital Grounds

• **Porous and Absorbent** - Watercolor paper, printmaking paper, Rice Paper, and so many of the other interesting handmade papers available today, as well as unpainted canvas, wallpapers, thin leather, and unsealed wood veneer.

• **Non-Porous** - Metallic specialty papers, aluminum foil, thin metal sheets (copper, for example), Mylar, Lexan, Plexiglas, and acetate.

• **Make-Your-Own Surfaces** - Here is where your amazing brain can really exercise itself. Any surface that you paint with acrylic paints can be printed on as well. OR, make a surface out of acrylic paint as a 'skin' (i.e. a gel or paint 'skin' the size of a piece of paper so you can run it through your printer).

Orange Rose printed on Black cardstock coated with Digital Ground White (Matte).
Cats photo printed onto collaged canvas coated with Digital Ground Clear Non-Porous.
Fish image printed onto handmade paper coated with Digital Ground Clear (Gloss).
Pelican image (copyright free) printed onto handmade patterned paper coated with Digital Ground White (Matte). Note how the pattern recedes.
Digital Image printed onto painted canvas coated with Digital Ground Clear (Gloss), fixed with spray varnish, and then embellished.
Multiple Photo Images printed onto painted canvas, coated with Digital Ground Clear (Gloss), fixed with spray varnish, and then embellished with painted details.

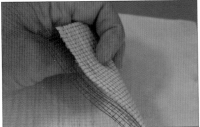

Create Your Own Surface Using Acrylic Products
Descriptions of 'Skins'

1. and 2. Print from a Computer: This flower image (copyright free) was printed directly from my Inkjet printer onto a flexible 'skin' I made and cut to 8½" by 11" to fit through my sheet feeder. It was prepped with Digital Ground White before printing. After it was printed I fixed the surface with a coat of Spray Varnish before adding more blue to the background to cover up the white ground.

3. Fiber Paste 'Skin': This is how the 'skin' looks after it is primed with the Digital Ground White, but before it is printed. I use netting or cheesecloth to anchor some of the product to the 'skin' when I am making them. You can see it in the 'skin'.

4. Crackled 'Skin': To make this interesting 'skin' you will need to do the following: Tape off an 8½" x 11" area on a level surface covered with HDPE or a Teflon Craft Sheet.

Spread a thin layer of Self-Leveling Clear Gel inside the taped area and just over the edges of the tape. Allow to dry into a clear 'skin'. Spread a thin layer of Crackle Paste on top of the Self-Leveling Clear Gel 'skin' and allow this layer to dry and form cracks. Lightly tint the Crackle Paste using a wash of Fluid Acrylic Paint.

Don't overwet the surface. Dry thoroughly before adding a final layer of Self-Leveling Clear Gel to trap the Crackle Paste. Essentially you have made a sandwich. If you want a non-glossy surface, apply one thin coat of Matte Medium.

When completely dry, trim off tape and treat with Digital Ground Clear for Non-Porous Surfaces. Select your image and print away!

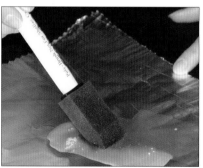

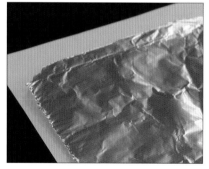

How To Prepare Your Surface for Printing

1. Cut your surface to fit your printer (most home printers are 8?" x 11" feed sheet size). Here I used a piece of kitchen foil and trimmed it to 8" x 10".

2. Using a foam brush, apply a thin coat of Digital Ground Clear for Non-Porous Surfaces, in one direction. Allow this first coat to dry. Brush on a second coat in the opposite direction. Allow this coat to dry also.

Note: This cross-coverage insures that all areas of the sheet receive a coating evenly.

3. Tape the metal foil to a heavy piece of paper with blue painters' tape.

4. Select your image, size it for printing, and print.

Printing on Metal - Palm Tree

Imagine printing on metal foil on your home computer! Digital Ground Clear for Non-Porous Surfaces makes it possible. This example was printed on 30 gauge metal. The embossed tooling was added after the image was printed.

A Note About Digital Ground

All of the Digital Grounds Products are Water-soluble so they are compatible with inkjet inks. What does that mean for you as an artist? If you are considering using these products in a layered piece with other paints and collage elements added onto the surface of the digital print, then you Must apply one or more layers of archival varnish, such as Golden's between the inkjet print and the future layers to "fix" or "seal" the surface before you add any additional layers.

The number of layers is related to the absorbency of the printable surface. Watercolor paper is more absorbent than tinfoil, for example, so you can have several layers of paint on the watercolor surface before you treat it with the Digital Media products. If once you have painted and embellished a piece and you decide you want to add additional inkjet embellishments, then you must re-prep the surface (two cross-brushed coats).

When it is dry it is once again ready to run through your printer to receive your images. You are, of course, limited by how thick the layers of your composition become as to whether or not the printer will feed properly.

Be Sure to 'Fix' the Layers -

If you forget to fix the layers, you will see your inkjet images "dissolve" when any wet product is applied. I learned this the hard way, so I'm sharing my knowledge with you in advance. Figure out some way to identify which coats are "fixed" so you don't get mixed up. I use a piece of low tack tape.

How to Use Your Printer

Whenever you have a doubt about whether your printable surface will pass easily through your inkjet printer, it's best to utilize a simple technique to anchor the surface to assist its passage through the printer. Use painters' tape to anchor the top and side edge of your surface to another piece of paper or, better yet, a transparency film.

By taping down these edges you will provide more stability to your surface (especially thin ones like foil or paint) and give your printer a straight firm edge to grab onto.

A Hint about Image Placement

Remember, the great thing about working with your home computer is that you can utilize the programs you already have to check alignment of your images and to copy and paste into a document.

Create your "composition" within the boundaries of a document. Then you can easily check alignment by printing out a dummy copy first and seeing if you are on the mark!

Purple Flowers (on canvas)

This digital image of purple geraniums was taken in my back yard. I printed it onto a painted paper canvas that was coated with Digital Ground Clear. After I fixed it with a coat of Spray Varnish, I embellished the piece with line details and additional pattern.

Figs (on paper)

I started with hand-painted watercolor paper which I treated with Digital Ground Clear and then printed with text using different sizes of type and fonts. I fixed that layer with Spray Varnish and proceeded to embellish with more paint.

Adding a second coat of Digital Ground Clear, I then ran it through the printer a second time adding the images of figs.

Once again I fixed the surface and completed my embellishments with large letter stamps plus collaged and painted details.

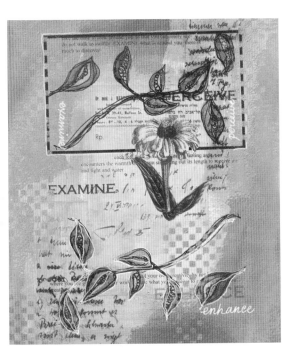

Flower & Vine (on paper)

This piece started out with painted and collaged watercolor paper which I treated with Digital Ground Clear before printing on computer generated text and drawings. They were fixed with Spray Varnish.

Finally, I added paint and collage embellishments.

Digital 'Faux' Transfers

Before I close out this brief introduction to these amazing products, I wanted to leave you with some images that I did when I began experimenting with Digital Grounds.

Because there are "multiple" layers on the pieces and because the computer allows for a seamlessness that is not possible with other processes, you won't be able to easily determine what is digital and what is "paint".

It is exactly that idea that I want you to imagine as you venture into this new arena. I hope you will enjoy the adventure as much as I do.

When Mistakes Become Opportunities

We cannot possibly try all these techniques without leaving behind a trail of failed attempts. That is the normal path for learning. It is through the trial and error process that we learn best.

So, I want to devote just a bit of space to how we can salvage our failed transfers and create something worthy of our efforts.

Opportunity #1
Failed Transfer as an Overpainting

I captured this digital image of a wild iris while on a trip to Florida.

I do not claim to be good at drawing, so I seized upon the ghostly transfers left on my canvases and grabbed my paints to "overpaint" the iris and turn failures into something I can really enjoy. By following the lines left behind and using the photo as a reference I created two contemporary interpretations of that moment at sunset in the Florida bog.

A "failed" transfer can easily create an opportunity for transformation, rather than trash!

Once I added transparent colors to this failed transfer, it began to take on a life of its own.

Start looking for the interesting lines and spaces that can be found in the broken and worn areas left where the transfer is incomplete.

1. Original digital Image of an iris.
2. I attempted to do an inkjet Soft Gel transfer (one of the quickie ones) and I was too impatient, so only the faintest of images remained behind.

A second painting created out of a transfer of the same image that was too light. With the addition of Fluid Acrylic color and an interesting treatment to the background it becomes transformed.

1. This is the original image that was transferred.
2. Here is the outcome of the transfer. Note that some areas didn't transfer well. I used a thick paper and I think I didn't have enough contact between the paper and the Acrylic product.

Opportunity #2
Incomplete Transfer as the Background

I attempted to transfer this image of a rose. I must tell you that most of my failures are due to impatience with the waiting time. It was a fairly large transfer and only parts of it took well.

But I could see the potential in the spaces left blank and proceeded to select and apply other images using various transfer processes to the board and by the time I was done I was very satisfied.

1. This is the second image that was used on the 'Faces' piece.
2. Here is the photo of the face. I enhanced the contrast and played with the color in my photo editing program.

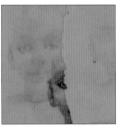

3. You can see 2 of the three transfer prints I made for this piece. The first is very ghostly, because I didn't wait long enough for the color to transfer.
4. In this picture I am pulling away the backing from the third transfer.
5. Here are the three faces with some color washing on the background.

Opportunity #3
Saving a 'Ghost Image'

I spotted this amazing wooden head in a display at a winery on a trip. It was too wonderful not to capture on my digital camera. I came home, pumped up the contrast and forced the head into a "face" that was quite dramatic. I wanted to do some inkjet Soft Gel transfers with it.

My first take was poorly timed and left me a very faint ghost. So I printed off a couple more images and overlapped them to create a more ethereal mood. I added a few pieces of a digitally altered photo of roses I took (torn up for collaged effect) a little paint, and here it is.

Making Transfers Work for You

Chris Cozen

Chris is an artist with an innate understanding of color and design. She has 30 years of experience in teaching and program planning. Chris has learned that using one's creativity to approach problem-solving makes things go much easier. She utilizes this skill to develop opportunities for her students to "discover" their own creative abilities.

She devotes her time and energy to the creative process. As a Working Artist for Golden Acrylic Colors, Chris finds her background to be a perfect complement when lecturing, teaching, or designing a class about acrylic painting materials and techniques.

Chris's favorite students are those that come with either no experience or a bias "against" acrylic! Her affiliation with Golden has really influenced her work, pushing her to explore new processes and materials.

Her studio is brimming with pieces that tell stories about people, many enriched with pieces of family history. Collage and mixed media pieces lively with color, texture and movement dominate her studio walls.

She conducts workshops throughout southern California and is a member of the Los Angeles Experimental Artists Group. Chris lives in California with her husband Darrell, where she enjoys a wonderful garden filled with roses and fruit trees, plentiful sunshine, a few cats and the company of friends. She has two married daughters.

Since 2000, Chris has exhibited at Memphis, Nashville, The A.E. Backus Gallery in Florida, and the Chapelle des Penitents in Callian, France. Her work is held in private collections in California, Maryland, Tennessee, Florida, Canada, Germany, France, Israel, and Norway.

Visit **www.goldenpaints.com** for more information about products and to see what classes are being offered in your area.

I've shared with you as many Transfer techniques as I could manage, but a book on Acrylic transfers would not be complete without a few ideas about embellishing them.

Making transfers and figuring out how to use them in artwork is only part of the equation. Technically you could just transfer something and leave it at that... essentially making a copy of something that already exists. The "Art" part comes in after you have transferred your images, either successfully or with mistakes.

What you do with the transfers, how you make them mesh with your own artistic expression; that is where making "Art" comes in.

Using Transfers to Transform Failed Paintings

Believe it or not, underneath this painting of a vintage dress and jewelry is a completely different painting that just never came together. There were some wonderful areas of relatively "lacy" textures which inspired me to over-paint the entire surface with Fluid Titan Buff, blocking only the previous colors while maintaining the texture I liked.

I then transferred the dress image into the corner and began the process of "re-building" the painting, choosing colors and adding additional textures to support the old-fashioned feeling the image inspired. In the end I added some stamped words, some writing, and of course, the "jewels" with Iridescent Pearl and Interference Violet Fluid Acrylic paint drops.

Embellishing with Paint

Since this book is more about Acrylic transfers, then using Acrylic products to enhance or unify your transfers is a good place to start. I highly recommend that you have a good selection of Fluid Acrylic Paints on hand, especially those with transparent pigments. Here are some of my favorites which make a great "starter" palette: Quinacridone Magenta, Turquois Phthalo, Nickel Azo Yellow.

With these three colors you can make an awesome green, a fabulous burnt orange, and a great purple. They mix together flawlessly and create beautiful glazes when mixed with Acrylic Glazing Liquid in a formula of 1 part paint to 10 parts Acrylic Glazing Liquid for the sheerest of colors.

If you don't have any of the Iridescent Fluid colors in your collection, I recommend Iridescent Bright Gold (Fine) for the palette I mentioned. And Micaceous Iron Oxide because it will mix well with all of the colors and provide beautiful glazes both when used plain and when one of the colors is added.

The transparent pigments will not get muddy or cloudy during your mixing as long as you keep them away from opaque colors. But they will tint your favorite whites (mine are Titanium White and Titan Buff) beautifully when you want opaque tints. You can easily create pink, aqua, lavender, light green, soft yellowish green, salmon, etc. with the same colors I mentioned above.

If you want to add others, then try Hansa Yellow Medium, Manganese Blue Hue, and Sap Green Hue, any of the Quinacridones, or Phthalos, Pyrrole Reds and Oranges, and Dioxazine Purple. For accent colors invest in a couple of Opaque pigments that will sit on top of the surface. My favorite is Cobalt Teal, but I also like Chromium Oxide Green, and Naples Yellow Hue.

Mixed Media and Transfers - Close-up detail of mixed transfers